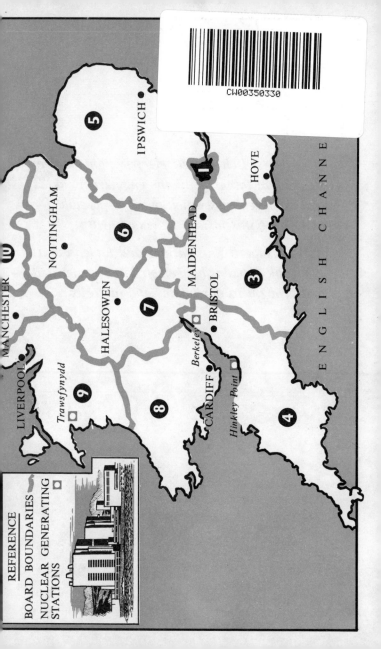

ENGLISH CHANNEL

IPSWICH

HOVE

MAIDENHEAD

NOTTINGHAM

MANCHESTER

BRISTOL

HALESOWEN

Berkeley

LIVERPOOL

CARDIFF

Trawsfynydd

Hinkley Point

REFERENCE

BOARD BOUNDARIES
NUCLEAR GENERATING
STATIONS

CW00350330

A Ladybird Book
Series 606E

*As we switch on our electric light or fire,
we seldom think of all the engineering skills
and achievements which make it possible for
us to have this instant light and heat.*

*With superb illustrations and a clear text,
this book explains how electricity is generated
and brought to our homes and factories.*

The Public Services
ELECTRICITY
A Ladybird 'Easy-Reading' Book

by I. & J. HAVENHAND

with illustrations by
JOHN BERRY

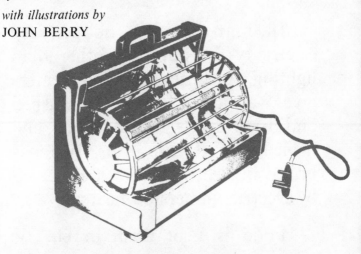

Publishers: Ladybird Books Ltd . Loughborough
© Ladybird Books Ltd (formerly Wills & Hepworth Ltd) 1966
Printed in England

SUPPLYING OUR ELECTRICITY

Fifty years ago our streets were badly lit and so were our homes. To-day, because of electricity there has been a great change. Our towns and homes are well lit, and we have electric power to help us in many ways.

In many homes people use electricity for purposes other than lighting. Electric fires and heaters give warmth. Clothes are washed and dried by electric machines and ironed with electric irons. Water is boiled in electric kettles and heated by electric immersion heaters.

Food is kept fresh in electric refrigerators, and cooked on electric cookers. Beds are warmed by electric blankets.

4

7214 0087 6

BLANKET

VACUUM CLEANER

LIGHT

ATER HEATER

FIRE

IRON

TOASTER

REFRIGERATOR

KETTLE

Without electricity we could not enjoy radio or television. Electricity is used to send out the programmes as well as to work the sets in our homes. Electric power is used in factories to drive machinery.

We have grown used to electricity. We do not think of the people whose work it is to see that electricity is there when we press a switch. The only person whom we see is the man who comes to read our electricity meter.

The illustration shows one of the latest types of meter which can be read outside the house.

Most things around us carry a small amount of electricity. Even our bodies make small electric currents.

After using a nylon comb we can make our hair stand on end by holding the comb above it.

Blow up a long balloon and rub it on your pullover. Place the balloon on the wallpaper and the electric charge in it will make it stay there.

Lightning that flashes across the sky is electricity, made by movement inside clouds. So much electricity is made that it flashes across to other clouds or down to the ground.

Over a hundred years ago, in 1831, a man called Michael Faraday discovered that he could make electricity pass through a wire. He moved some wire between the ends of magnets and found that this made an electric current. This showed him that electricity could be made and controlled by man.

To-day we use the same idea only we find it easier to keep the wire still and turn the magnets. As long as we can keep magnets turning inside coils of wire we can make all the electricity we want.

All the electricity that we use is made by the Central Electricity Generating Board, at power stations in different parts of the country.

The machines that make electricity are called generators. At an electric power station there are many of these huge generators.

The coils of wire are held firmly in place inside steel cases. In the middle of the coils of wire are magnets. The magnets are made to turn at very fast speeds.

To make the magnets turn, some other kind of power must be used.

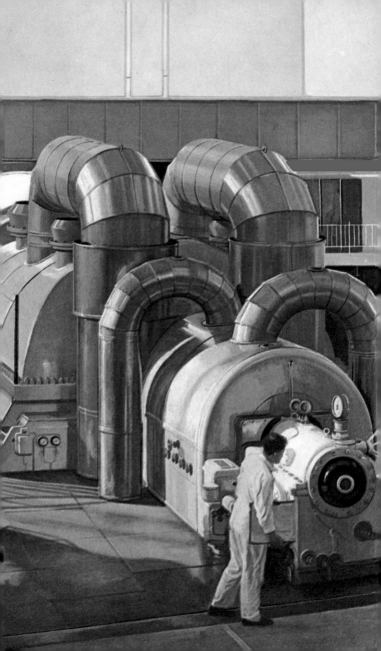

To get the power that is needed to drive generators, we can use water, coal, oil or uranium. Uranium is used to make atomic power.

When coal, oil or uranium are used they are made to give out heat. This heat is used to change water into steam. The steam is then used to run machines called steam turbines, and these turn the generators.

Water power can be very cheap and is used where there are rivers flowing through mountainous country. Water always flows downhill and as it flows it can be used to turn wheels.

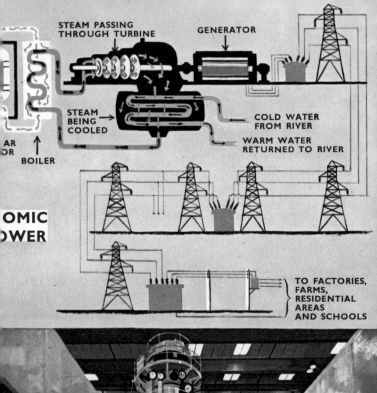

STEAM PASSING THROUGH TURBINE

GENERATOR

...AR ...OR

BOILER

STEAM BEING COOLED

COLD WATER FROM RIVER

WARM WATER RETURNED TO RIVER

OMIC OWER

TO FACTORIES, FARMS, RESIDENTIAL AREAS AND SCHOOLS

...DE AN ATOMIC ...ER STATION

Hydro means water, and so electricity made by water power is made at Hydro-electric Power Stations.

A dam is made across a valley and this holds back the water and stores it in a reservoir. The water can be used at any time. It flows through very large pipes to the power station, built near the bottom of the dam.

The water turns wheels built into the ends of the pipes. These are called water turbines and they drive the electric generators.

TURBINE TURNED BY WATER
WORKS THE ELECTRIC GENERATOR

At Ffestiniog in North Wales the Central Generating Board has tried out a new idea for storing power to drive the generators.

Two dams and two reservoirs have been made, a high and a low one of each. When a lot of electricity is needed the water from the top reservoir is allowed to flow down through the pipes. The water turns the turbines and the generators make electricity. The water then runs into the lower reservoir.

During the night not much electricity is being used. Some of the spare electricity from other power stations is used to drive pumps. These pump the water up to the top reservoir, ready to be used again.

We have plenty of coal in our country and much of it is used for making electricity.

Coal-fired power stations are built near coal-fields or where coal can be carried to them cheaply.

The coal is crushed to a fine dust and is blown by warm air into the furnaces. The furnaces are underneath the boilers where the steam is made. This steam is made hotter, to make it more powerful. It is then used to drive the steam turbines which drive the generators.

The steam is cooled and turned back into water in a 'condenser', from which it is pumped back into the boiler.

Sometimes the boilers are heated by burning oil instead of coal.

The Central Electricity Generating Board is always looking for cheaper and better ways of making electricity.

Nuclear or atomic power stations, like the one in the picture, have been built to use the power of the atom. Atoms are the smallest particles which make up everything around us. When atoms are split, they split other atoms and this gives heat. The heat is used to make a gas hot. The hot gas heats water to make steam. The steam is used to drive the steam turbines which turn the generators.

At every power station there is a control room. The generators and high voltage switches are all worked from the control room. Dials and lights on the control panels show the engineer on duty what is happening to machinery all over the power station.

The controlling engineer can stop or start generators so that enough electricity is being made at any time.

The country is divided into areas and each one has a Control Centre, where it is decided how much electricity each power station must generate.

In the picture you see the men at the National Control Centre in London, where they work out how much electricity will be needed next day for the whole country.

The men read the weather forecast to see if it will be cold. They even look at the television programmes to see if people will be staying up late.

When they have worked out how much electricity will be needed they telephone the engineers at the Area Control Centres. The engineers then telephone the power stations and tell them how many generators are to work on the next day.

Some of the electricity that we use is loaned to us by France. At times we need extra electricity when there is some to spare in France.

When we have spare electricity and France needs some, we pay back the electricity that we have borrowed.

In this way both countries help each other. It has also saved both countries from building generators which would not be needed all the time.

Two cables, thirty miles long, run under the sea from England to France. The electricity passes along these cables.

ENGLAND

CHANNEL

N

30 MILES

ENGLISH

FRANCE

When we turn on a water tap, water comes out because other water is pushing it out. This is called water pressure. Electric current flows through wires because it is being pushed along.

The pressure of electricity is called voltage. The pressure or voltage in the wires in our homes is about 240 volts.

When the electricity is made by the generators it is about 11,000 volts. Even this is not enough to send it long distances, so the electricity must first pass through a transformer.

Transformers can make the current either stronger or weaker.

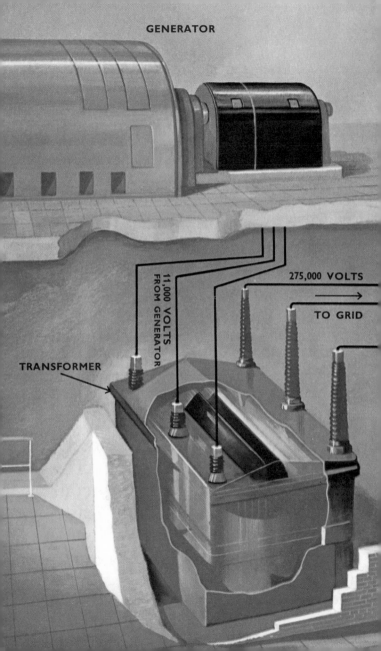

GENERATOR

11,000 VOLTS FROM GENERATOR

275,000 VOLTS

TO GRID

TRANSFORMER

The transformers at the generating stations change the voltage from 11,000 volts to 132,000 volts or 275,000 volts. Soon a higher voltage of 400,000 volts will be used.

When the electricity leaves the transformer it goes into the grid. The grid is the network of cables and wires which are spread across the country. This grid carries the electricity from the generating stations to villages, towns and cities that will use it.

Whenever possible, generating stations are built near coal-fields or reservoirs, and the electricity distributed by the grid. This is cheaper than carrying coal to generating stations built near cities and towns which are a long way from coal-fields and reservoirs.

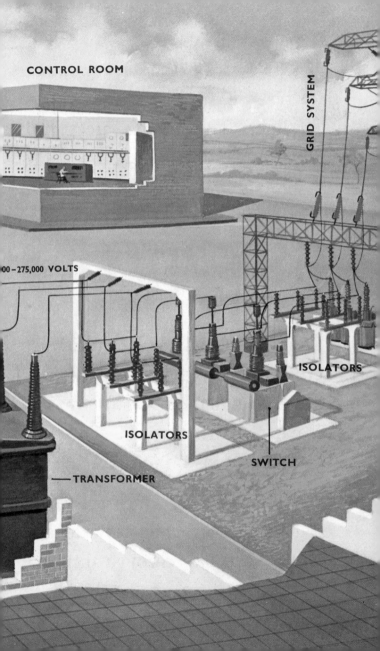

CONTROL ROOM

GRID SYSTEM

00—275,000 VOLTS

ISOLATORS

ISOLATORS

SWITCH

— TRANSFORMER

The wires that carry the electricity in the grid must be strong and light. These wires are called transmission lines. They are made of aluminium, which is light and carries electricity well. The aluminium wires are mixed with steel wires, to make the transmission lines strong.

The transmission lines are carried across the country on tall steel pylons. So that no electricity can escape from the wires, they are hung from the pylons on insulators.

The insulators, which are made of glass or porcelain (pot), do not let electricity pass through them.

Some lengths of new transmission lines are very difficult to build. The pylons may have to be built in countryside where there are no roads. All the girders for the pylons have to be carried to the place where the pylon will be built.

The wires have to go over woods, valleys and rivers. Rockets are used to carry a thin line over these places. The thin line is then used to pull the transmission wires into place. Helicopters are often used to carry the girders and wires over long, difficult stretches of country.

High voltage transmission lines are carried overhead on pylons because it would cost a lot more money to lay them underground.

Electricity from the grid is much too powerful for us to use in our homes and factories. Near towns the transmission lines take the electricity to sub-stations.

At the sub-stations the pressure of the electricity is stepped down through transformers. Underground cables now carrying 11,000 volts take the electricity from these sub-stations into towns. Here, at smaller sub-stations, the electricity is transformed down to 240 volts so that we can use it in our homes.

To carry the electricity to our homes, cables are taken from the local sub-stations. These cables are buried under nearly all the pavements in our towns.

The cables are buried in trenches about three feet deep. When the cables have been covered with earth, concrete slabs are put over the top of them and the trenches are then filled in.

The concrete slabs prevent the cables being hit by the picks and shovels of other workmen who may have to dig under the pavements.

Sometimes cables have to be joined. Other cables may have to be split to carry electricity to different parts of a town or into houses.

Every wire in the cables must be perfectly joined. When the wires have been joined, care must be taken that water and damp cannot get to them. The electricity could leak away through the damp area.

To keep a joint dry it is covered first with insulating tape. This is then covered with melted pitch. When the pitch sets hard it makes a water-proof cover.

Just before the electric cable reaches the meter in our homes, there is a main fuse box. A fuse is made of special wire which can carry only a certain amount of electricity. If something goes wrong, the fuse wire burns away and cuts off the electricity.

The meter measures all the electricity that we use. When we switch on anything electrical, a wheel inside the meter begins to turn. The more electricity we use, the faster the wheel turns.

When the wheel has turned a number of times, it moves the fingers on the clock faces.

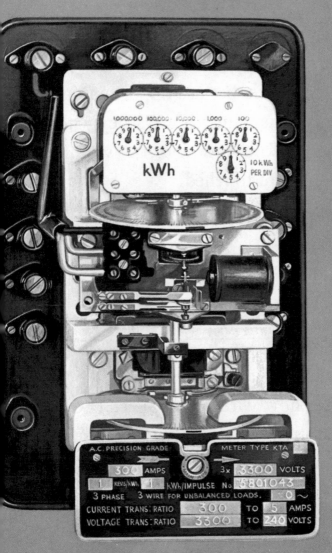

INSIDE AN ELECTRIC METER

Wires lead from the meter to large switch boxes with fuses in them. These switches are important, as the electricity must always be switched off before any electric wiring or fuses are touched.

Other wires go from the switch boxes to carry electricity to lighting points and power points all over the house.

In some houses each of these wires has a separate fuse. New houses are now wired with special sockets so that only plugs with a fuse in them will fit. This is a very good way to help make electricity safe to use.

YOU MUST <u>NEVER</u> TOUCH ANY OF THESE

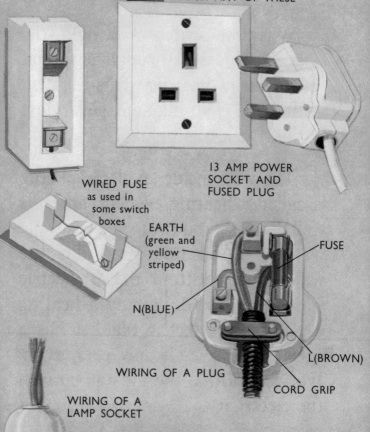

13 AMP POWER SOCKET AND FUSED PLUG

WIRED FUSE as used in some switch boxes

EARTH (green and yellow striped)

FUSE

N(BLUE)

L(BROWN)

WIRING OF A PLUG

CORD GRIP

WIRING OF A LAMP SOCKET

13 AMP FUSE

ELECTRIC FIRE, WASHING MACHINE, WATER HEATER, ETC.

3 AMP FUSE

KETTLE, TOASTER, IRON, VACUUM CLEANER, REFRIGERATOR, SPIN DRYER, BLANKET, T.V. SET, RADIO, LIGHTING, ETC.

When we switch on a light, the electricity passes through a special thin wire in the bulb. This is called a filament. The filament gets white hot and gives us light.

The wire inside an electric kettle is called a heating element, and it is well covered and protected from the water. It gets hot and boils the water. The bottom of an electric iron is also made hot by a heating element. An electric blanket has a special wire which only gets warm. If it gets hot, a 'thermostat' cuts off the electricity.

The electricity we use may have come a long way from a power station to give us light, heat and power.

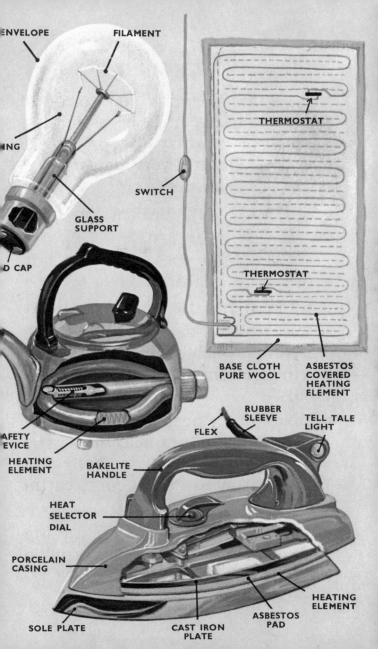

ENVELOPE

FILAMENT

NG

GLASS SUPPORT

SWITCH

D CAP

THERMOSTAT

THERMOSTAT

SAFETY DEVICE

HEATING ELEMENT

BASE CLOTH PURE WOOL

ASBESTOS COVERED HEATING ELEMENT

FLEX

RUBBER SLEEVE

TELL TALE LIGHT

BAKELITE HANDLE

HEAT SELECTOR DIAL

PORCELAIN CASING

SOLE PLATE

CAST IRON PLATE

ASBESTOS PAD

HEATING ELEMENT

SAFETY FIRST!

Anything that is connected to mains electricity must be used with care. We cannot see or smell electricity, but it is very dangerous—electricity can kill!

Never touch broken or bare wires.

If anything goes wrong do not touch it—switch off.

Never try to mend electrical things yourself.

Never touch switches, plugs or anything electrical with wet or damp hands.

Never play near or climb pylons, and do not fly kites near them. The electricity could use your body and the kite string as a short cut to earth, and could kill you!

The children in the picture are playing well away from the pylon and wires.

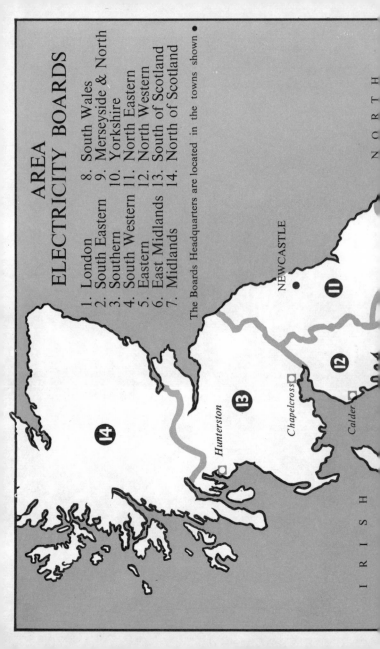

AREA
ELECTRICITY BOARDS

1. London
2. South Eastern
3. Southern
4. South Western
5. Eastern
6. East Midlands
7. Midlands
8. South Wales
9. Merseyside & North
10. Yorkshire
11. North Eastern
12. North Western
13. South of Scotland
14. North of Scotland

The Boards Headquarters are located in the towns shown ●

NEWCASTLE

Hunterston

Chapelcross

Calder

NORTH

IRISH